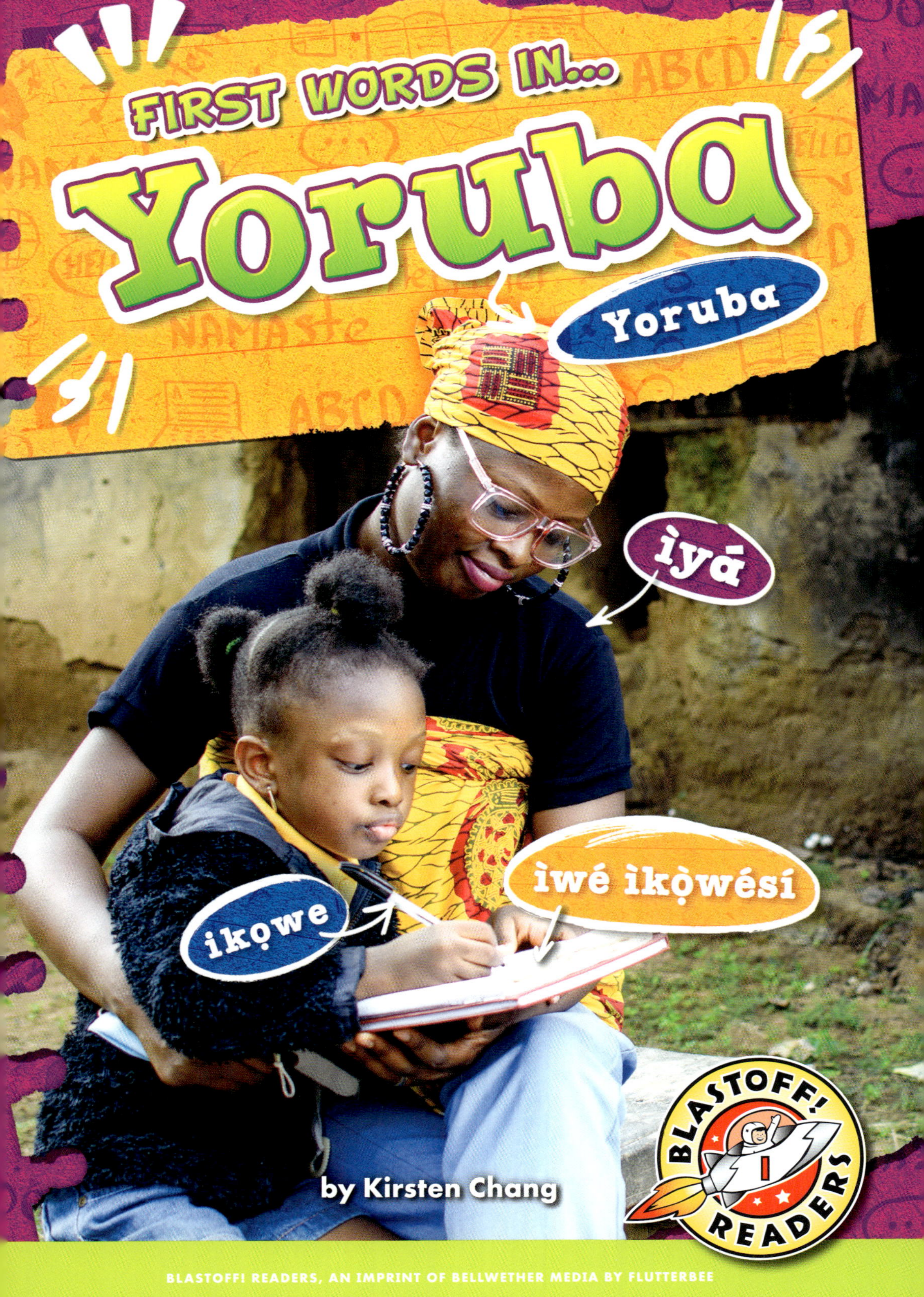
FIRST WORDS IN...
Yoruba
Yoruba
ìyá
ìwé ìkọ̀wésí
ikọwe
by Kirsten Chang
BLASTOFF! READERS
BLASTOFF! READERS, AN IMPRINT OF BELLWETHER MEDIA BY FLUTTERBEE

Blastoff! Readers are carefully developed by literacy experts to build reading stamina and move students toward fluency by combining standards-based content with developmentally appropriate text.

Level 1 provides the most support through repetition of high-frequency words, light text, predictable sentence patterns, and strong visual support.

Level 2 offers early readers a bit more challenge through varied sentences, increased text load, and text-supportive special features.

Level 3 advances early-fluent readers toward fluency through increased text load, less reliance on photos, advancing concepts, longer sentences, and more complex special features.

★ **Blastoff! Universe**

Reading Level

Grade K

Grades 1–3

Grade 4

This edition first published in 2026 by Bellwether Media, Inc.

For information regarding permission, write to Bellwether Media, Inc., Attention: Permissions Department, 3500 American Blvd W, Suite 150, Bloomington, MN 55431.

Library of Congress Cataloging-in-Publication Data is available at www.loc.gov or upon request from the publisher.

ISBN: 9798893047790 (hardcover)
ISBN: 9798893048797 (ebook)

Editor: Suzane Nguyen Designer: Andrea Schneider

Printed in the United States of America, North Mankato, MN.

Table of Contents

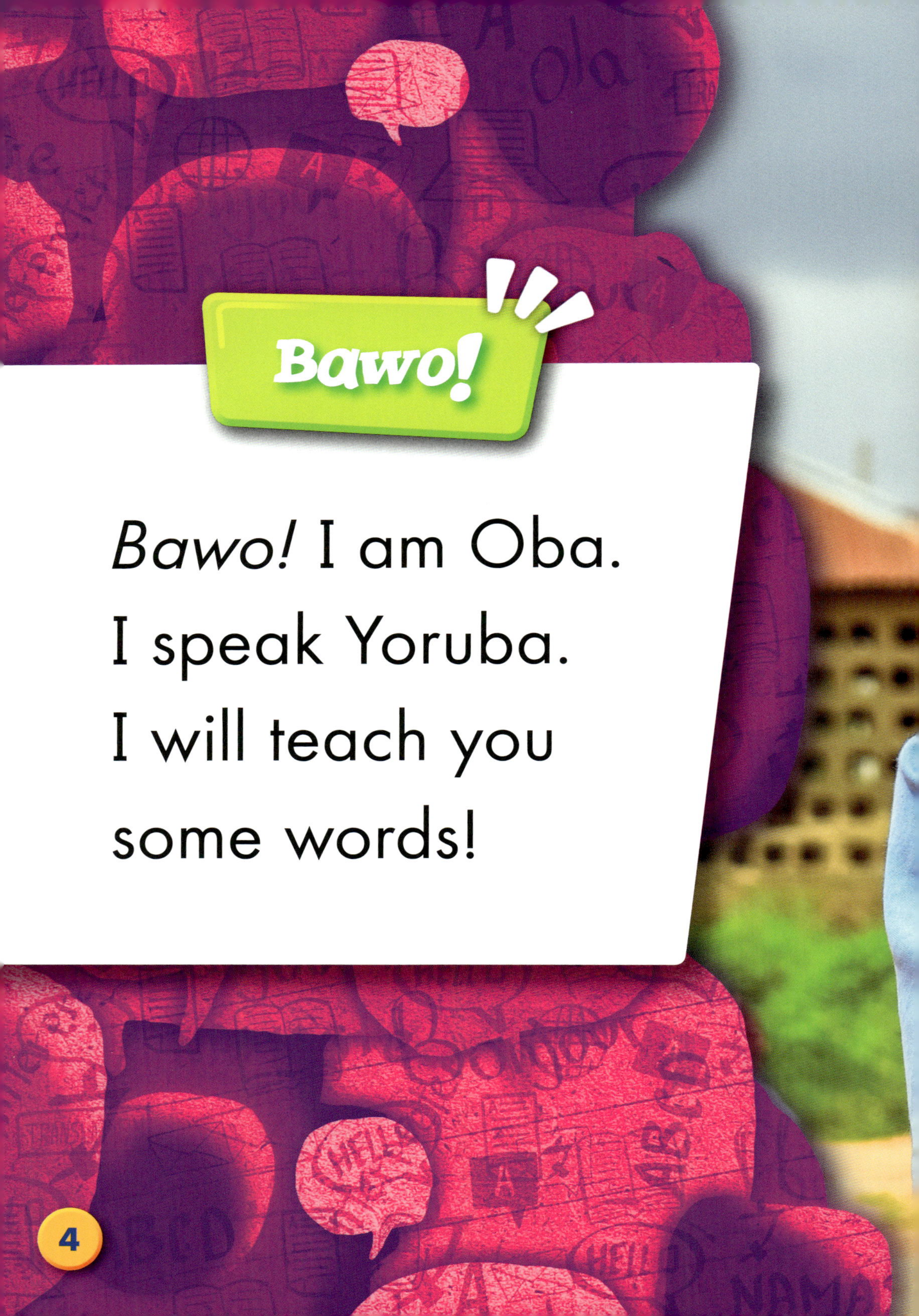

Bawo!

Bawo! I am Oba.
I speak Yoruba.
I will teach you
some words!

Words to Know

- ẹ káárọ = good morning
  (eh kah-ROH)
- bẹ́ẹ̀ni = yes
  (beh-nee)
- rárá = no
  (rah-rah)
- orúkọ mi ni = my name is
  (OH-ROO-koh mee nee)

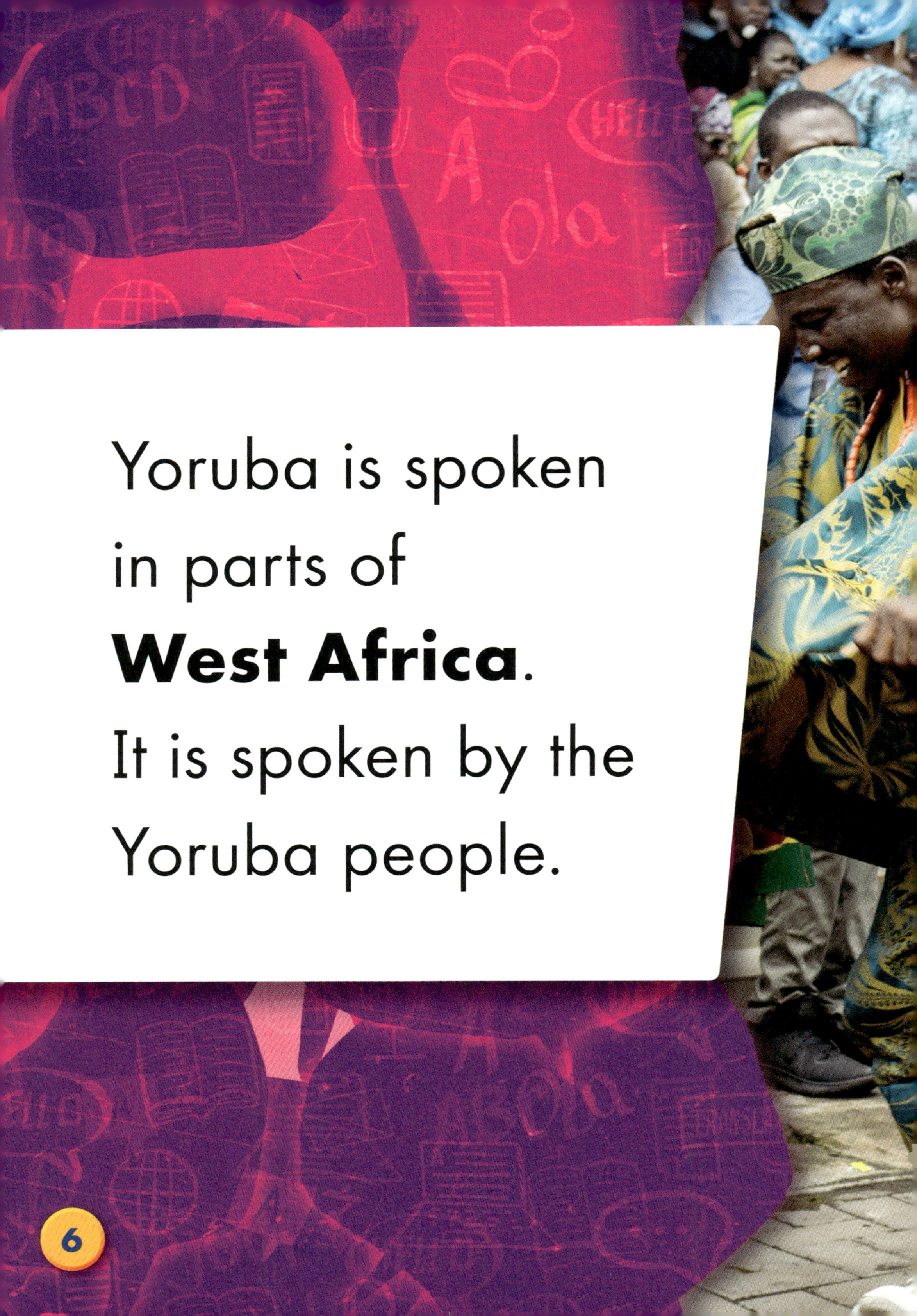

Yoruba is spoken in parts of **West Africa**. It is spoken by the Yoruba people.

Yoruba-speaking Countries
West Africa

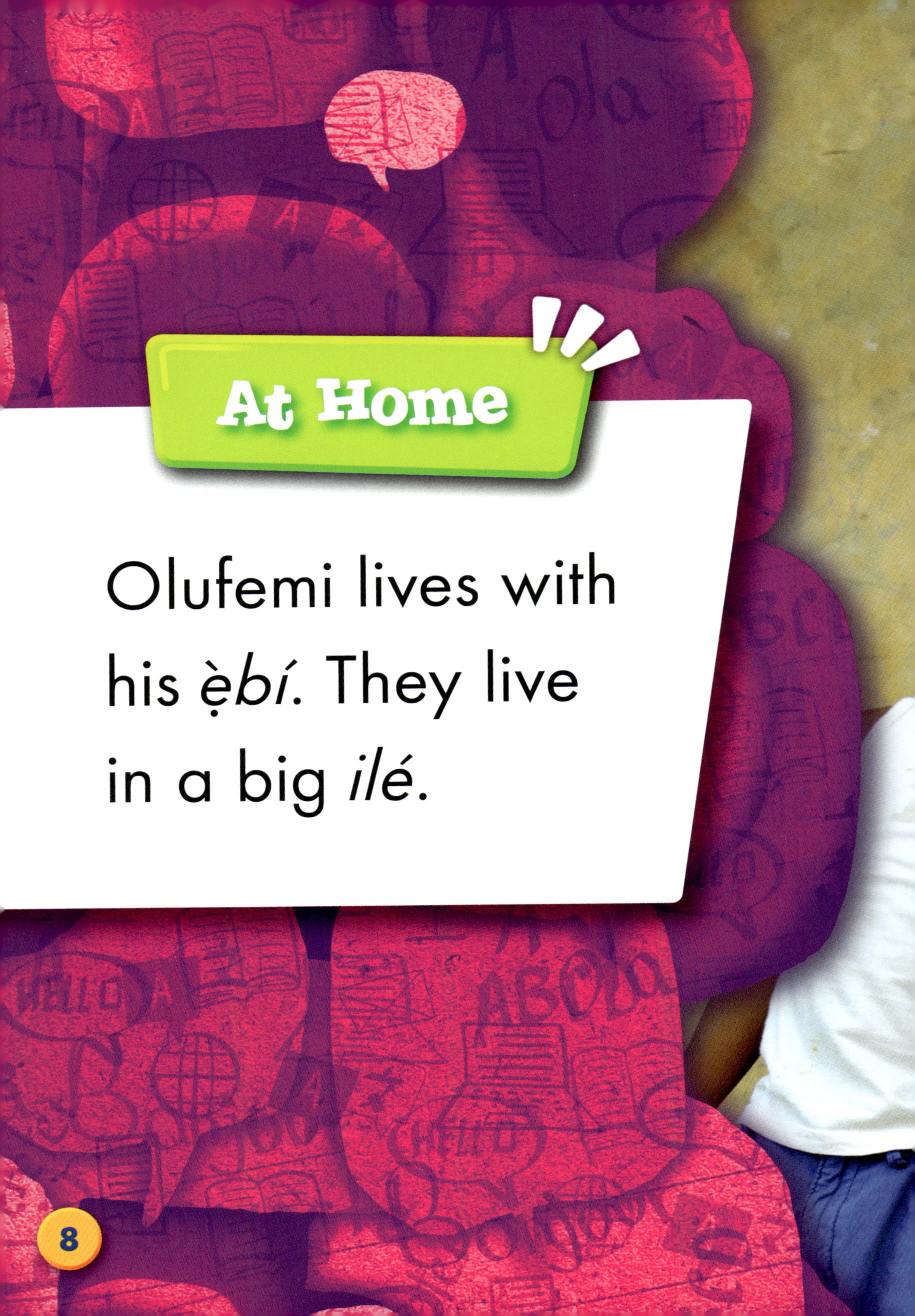

At Home

Olufemi lives with his *ẹ̀bí*. They live in a big *ilé*.

Words to Know

- èbí = **family** (eh-BEE)
- ilé = **house** (ee-LAY)
- bàbá = **father** (bah-BAH)
- ìyá = **mother** (ee-YAH)

It is *òwúrọ̀*. Adisa eats *oúnjẹ àárọ̀*. She loves **moi moi**!

oúnjẹ àárọ̀
Words to Know
• òwúrọ̀ = morning
(oh-woo-roh)
• oúnjẹ àárọ̀ = breakfast
(ohn-jay ah-roh)
• tábìlì = table
(tah-bee-lee)
• wàra = milk
(wah-rah)

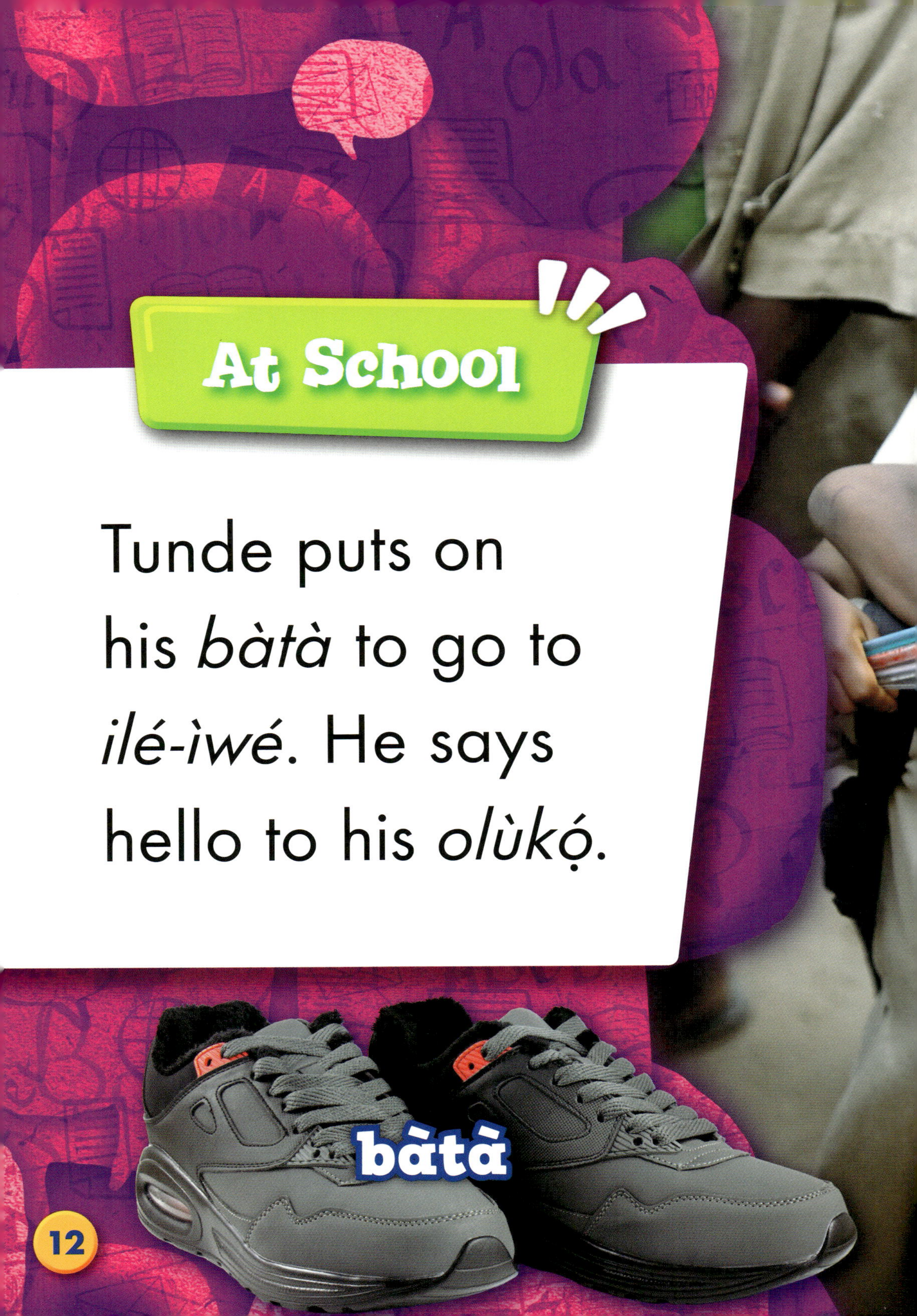

At School

Tunde puts on his *bàtà* to go to *ilé-ìwé*. He says hello to his *olùkọ́*.

Words to Know
• bàtà = shoes
(bah-TAH)
• ilé-ìwé = school
(ee-LAY ee-WAY)
• olùkọ́ = teacher
(oh-loo-KOH)
• apo = bag
(ah-PO)
apo

Taiwo reads an *ìwé* in class. Then he writes in his *ìwé ìkọ̀wésí*.

ìwé ìkọ̀wésí

Count in Yoruba

ọkan (OH-kahn).... 1
eji (AY-jee).................. 2
ẹta (EH-tah)........ 3
ẹrin (EH-reen)........... 4
arun (AH-roon)... 5
ẹfa (EH-fah)............ 6
eje (AY-jay).......... 7
ẹẹjọ (EH-joh)................ 8
ẹsan (EH-sahn)... 9
ẹwa (EH-wah)........... 10

Words to Know

- ìwé = **book** (ee-WAY)
- ikọwe = **pen** (ee-KOH-weh)
- yàrá ìkàwé = **classroom** (yah-RAH ee-kah-WAY)
- ìwé ìkọ̀wésí = **notebook** (ee-WAY ee-koh-way-SEE)

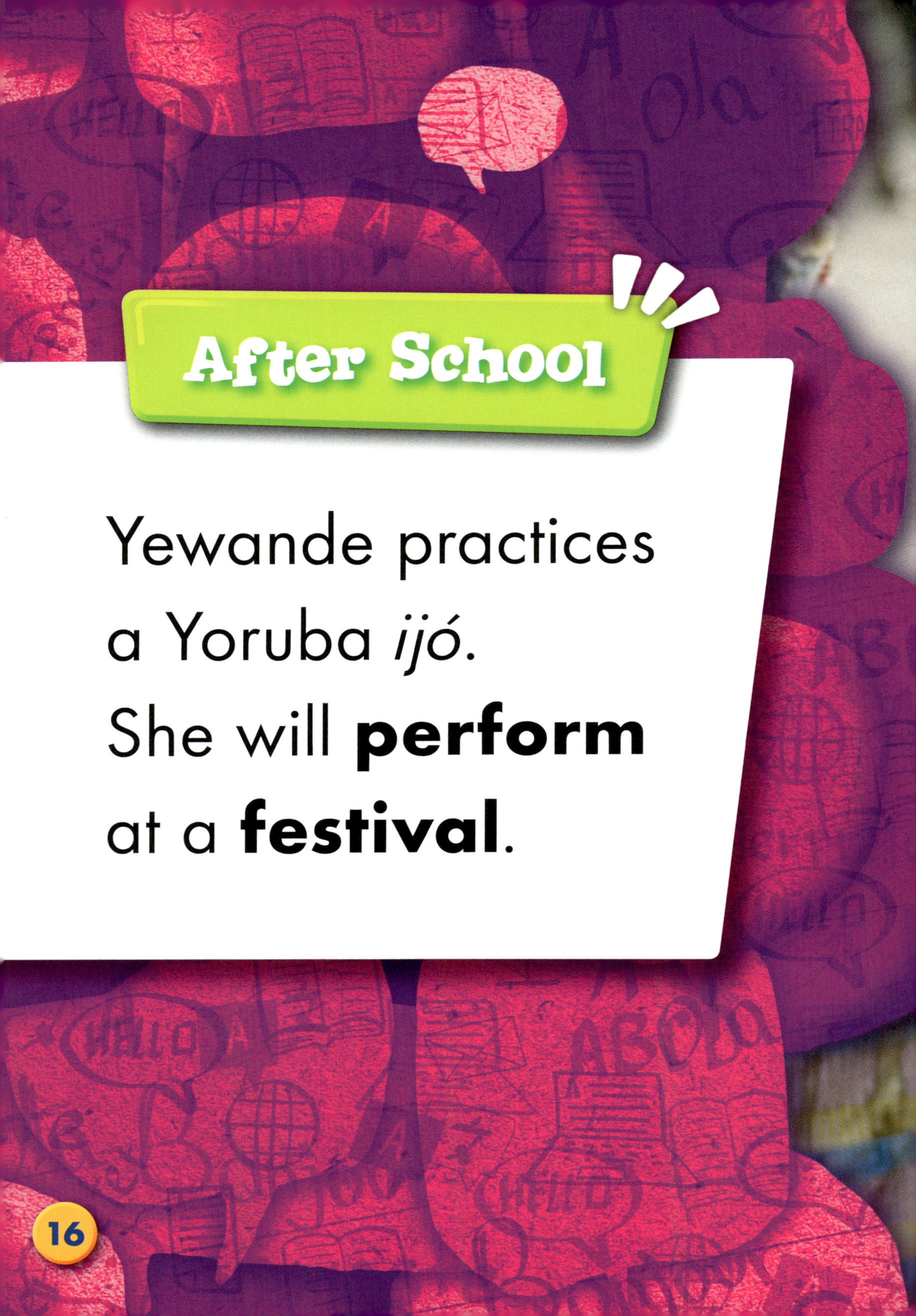

After School

Yewande practices a Yoruba *ijó*. She will **perform** at a **festival**.

aṣọ
Words to Know
• ijó = dance
(EE-joh)
• ìlù = drum
(EE-loo)
• orin = music
(oh-REEN)
• aṣọ = dress
(ah-SHAW)

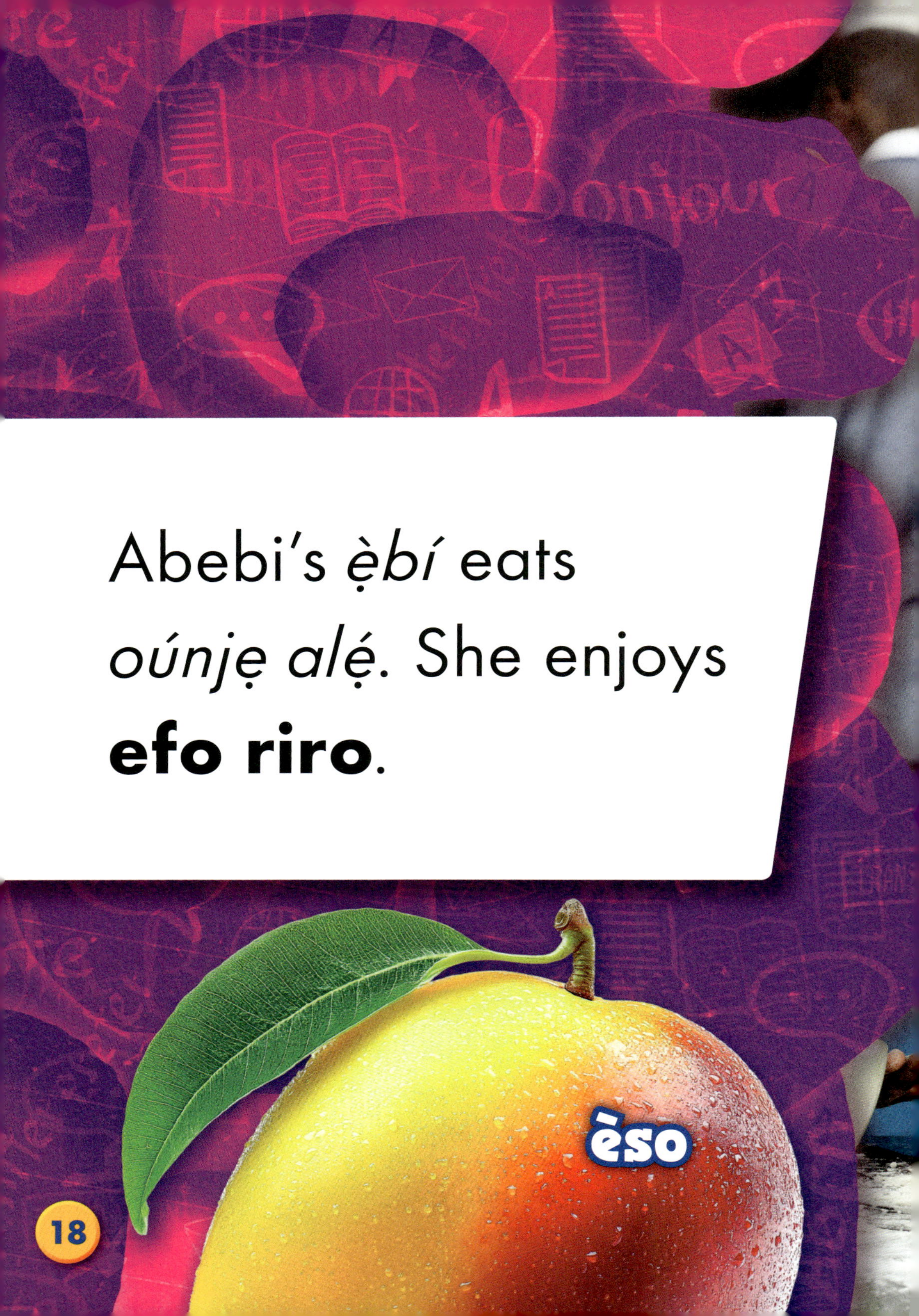

Abebi's *ẹ̀bí* eats *oúnjẹ alẹ́*. She enjoys **efo riro**.

Words to Know
• oúnjẹ alẹ́ = dinner
(OHN-jah ah-LAY)
• búrẹ́dì = bread
(boo-red-EE)
• wàràǹkàsì = cheese
(wah-rahn-kah-SEE)
• èso = fruit
(ay-SO)
oúnjẹ alẹ́

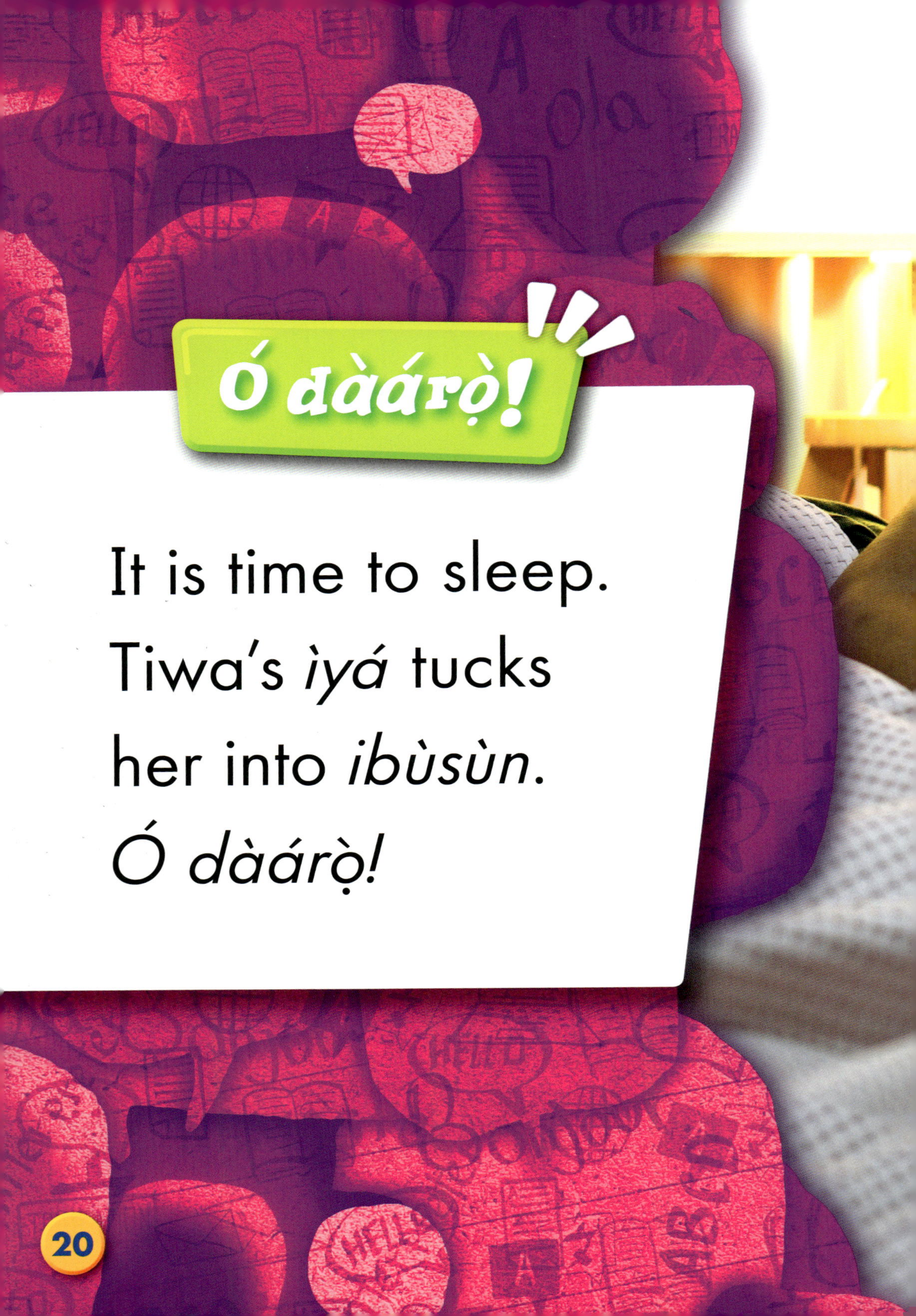

Ó dàárọ̀!

It is time to sleep. Tiwa's *ìyá* tucks her into *ibùsùn*. *Ó dàárọ̀!*

Words to Know

- ibùsùn = **bed**
  (EE-boo-soon)
- yàrá = **bedroom**
  (yah-RAH)
- fìtílà = **lamp**
  (fee-TEE-lah)
- ìrọ̀rí = **pillow**
  (ee-roar-EE)

Glossary

efo riro

a Yoruba spinach stew

perform

an action or activity that requires training and skill

festival

a time or event of celebration

West Africa

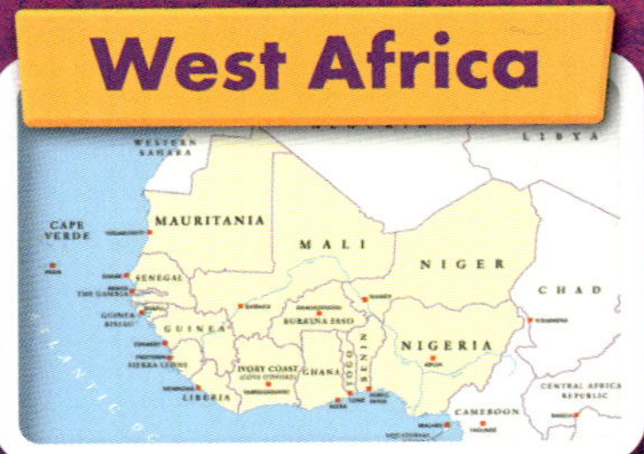

a region in western Africa made up of 16 countries

moi moi

a traditional Nigerian breakfast food made of steamed beans

To Learn More

AT THE LIBRARY

Langdo, Bryan. *Nigeria*. Minneapolis, Minn.: Bellwether Media, 2025.

Thorpe, Judy. *West African Cuisine*. Buffalo, N.Y.: Enslow Publishing, 2024.

Wilkins, Veronica B. *Explore Africa*. Minneapolis, Minn.: Jump!, 2020.

ON THE WEB

FACTSURFER

Factsurfer.com gives you a safe, fun way to find more information.

1. Go to www.factsurfer.com.
2. Enter "Yoruba" into the search box and click 🔍.
3. Select your book cover to see a list of related content.

Index

The images in this book are reproduced through the courtesy of: ehinde Olufemi Akinbo, front cover; Alucardion, p. 3; Oni Abimbola, pp. 4-5; Ajibola Fasola, pp. 6-7; ariyo Olasunkanmi, pp. 8-9; Joy Nnenna, p. 10 (moi moi); Stella_E, pp. 10-11; malshak_off, p. 12 (bàtà); Photononstop/ Alamy Stock Photo, pp. 12-13; photomelon, p. 14 (ìwé ìkọ̀wésí); commerceandculturestock/ Getty Images, pp. 14-15; David Levenson/ Alamy Stock Photo, pp. 16-17; Dien, p. 18 (èso); Greatstock/ Alamy Stock Photo, pp. 18-19; Iammotos, pp. 20-21; Red Confidential, p. 22 (efo riro); Fela Sanu, p. 22 (festival); Primestock Photography, p. 22 (moi moi); OMONIYI AYEDUN OLUBUNMI/ Alamy Stock Photo, p. 22 (perform); PeterHermesFurian, p. 22 (West Africa).